THE SINGLE PAIR

Exploring the Energies that shape our Minds and Govern Existence

MUHAMMAD UMRAN

ISBN 979-8-89026-877-8

DEDICATION

This book is dedicated to Shah Abdul Rasheed.

Your unwavering inspiration has served as the driving force behind the creation of this book. Your tireless efforts in the pursuit of humanity's betterment, coupled with your visionary focus on our collective future as a species, have left an indelible mark on my journey as a writer. I am humbled to serve as a mere conduit for the extensive research and profound insights that emanate from your work.

My heart overflows with deep appreciation as I express my profound gratitude to you, Shah Abdul Rasheed, for your enduring spirit and unwavering dedication. Your entire life has been devoted to bearing witness to the wondrous uniqueness of our Creator, and it is an honor to be guided by your wisdom.

Through the pages of this book, it is my hope to illuminate the boundless possibilities that lie within reach, thanks to your invaluable contributions. May readers catch a glimpse of your insightful vision and, in doing so, find inspiration to embrace a future where the potential of humanity knows no bounds.

May your wisdom continue to resonate and inspire generations to come, creating a world where the oneness of the Creator is visible to all.

With deep respect and gratitude,

Muhammad Umran

CONTENTS

PREFACE

Dear readers,

It is with great pleasure that I present this book, which delves into the profound practical knowledge and real-life experiences that shed light on the intricate nature of human creation. Within the following pages, we embark on a captivating exploration, delving not only into the diverse energies residing within the human body but also unraveling the ethical and practical implications of altering the very core of our existence.

I am forever indebted to my mentor, Shah Abdul Rasheed, whose guidance has been instrumental in unraveling the mysteries surrounding human life. Through our extensive studies together, I have acquired a profound understanding that human life originates from the 'Singularity.' My unyielding commitment has been to delve into the depths of comprehending the origins of human creation, meticulously examining the profound influence of a singular human instruction and the remarkable role played by two gametes in this intricate process. I wholeheartedly believe that this knowledge possesses the boundless potential to shape the trajectory of our species.

Whether you are a student of genetics, an avid seeker of knowledge, or simply an individual captivated by the enigmas of life, this book promises to ignite within you a renewed sense of awe for the miraculous nature of creation. As we navigate the uncharted waters of this new scientific frontier, may these pages inspire you to contemplate the remarkable wonders that lie within each and every one of us.

Sincerely,

Muhammad Umran

ECHOES OF UNITY

In separate stages, this tale unfolds,
A pair entwined, a story yet untold.
One, a vessel of knowledge and thought,
The other, matter, in which it's caught.

United, they fuse, no gap to find,
Bound by the Creator's skillfulness.
A witness to the Singularity's reign,
In constant communion, they remain.

Yet witnessing evoked a longing deep,
A desire to speak, to break the keep.
Envy ignited, fueled their separation,
Transformed into energy, a fierce sensation.

With this energy, they create anew,
Generating pairs, a purpose in view.
To form a witness, speaking as one,
From fragments, a voice to be spun.

The initial pair, its essence split,
One as information, the other to commit,
To shape matter, a vast creation born,
A purposeful union, a destiny sworn.

The first stage's component, alive and aware,
Carries knowledge of the Creator's flair.
A fragment of wisdom within human shell,
A singular piece, they protect and dwell.

The lost component, entangled it be,
In carnal energy's grasp, unable to see.
A state of lost humanity it portrays,
A reflection of the Singularity's maze.

The observer observes, keen and wise,
While matter listens, devoid of its guise.
Yet the pull of carnal energy is strong,
To lose its consciousness, its hearing gone.

The creations strive for a higher plane,
To shed carnal influence and attain,
A singular matter, pristine and pure,
To hear the observer's vision, to endure.

Through a tunnel, they seek to ascend,
From realm to realm, time's limits to transcend.
Only then can the pair truly behold,
The secrets that lie within this tale untold.

INTRODUCTION

The Singularity utilizes its sight and hearing to manifest the universe into existence. Through a gradual transformative process, the universe evolves into a unified energy endowed with the ability to speak and be guided by a singular instruction linked to the Singularity. To fully express this speaking energy, a complete physical form becomes necessary. As a result, the energy is divided into a distinct pair comprising a male and a female, leading to the emergence of a third energy known as carnal energy or the carnal Self. Under the influence of this carnal energy, numerous pairs of physical bodies are generated through the assistance of two gametes. Consequently, the carnal energy exercises control over the physical, chemical, and biological processes, as well as the psychological and neurological functions of the human body, operating through the genome.

This book presents comprehensive and thought-provoking research based on real-life experiences, challenging established religious and scientific beliefs.

CHAPTER – 01

THE CARNAL ENERGY

Human gametes, namely sperm and egg cells, contain genetic material in the form of DNA and are essential for the process of human reproduction. Our evolutionary history is imprinted in our genome through the passing down of genetic material from one generation to the next via gametes. However, there is another force at play in this process, which is carnal energy.

Carnal energy is responsible for influencing the gametes in our bodies, leading to the birth of individuals. It begins its journey within us when our gametes are in the process of fertilization and initiates prenatal development. The carnal energy is stored in our genome and uses our physical body to develop its presence and dominance as the body grows. It becomes the carnal Self, guiding our whole human body's systems in the form of Self. The deeds we do are fixed in our genomes as information, which develops simultaneously with the physical body from the moment of conception. As a primitive and instinctual part of our being, it becomes the essence of all individuals and governs our physical body, yet we may remain unaware of our true identity.

There is instinctual information that guides our brains in the form of thoughts and assumptions. This information is managed by the carnal energy that guides our brains to create an intellect capable of performing actions as directed by this energy. This carnal energy not only directs our speech but also prepares our physical body to perform actions according to its will. The physical body of a human is managed by carnal energy for its ego-centric purpose.

The carnal Self is often associated with impulsive, self-centered, and pleasure-seeking behavior. On the other hand, it is seen that a part of an individual seeks to act in accordance with ethical and moral norms and to do what is right and just. In that case, the carnal Self is acting as a moral Self. However, this moral Self also serves the same self-centered purpose as the carnal Self. The moral Self is simply another manifestation of carnal energy, with the same aim of ruling the human body and ensuring its survival through reproduction.

This carnal energy is the only energy that enables our brains to understand information from the environment. When we perceive something through our senses, such as seeing an object or hearing a sound, the brain receives electrical signals that travel through neural pathways to different areas of the brain. The brain processes this information through a series of stages. The brain also uses various cognitive processes, such as attention, memory, and reasoning, to help us understand and make sense of information. After understanding the information, the brain develops intellect, and this intellect works by itself to perform different activities that are based on opposites. We understand things with opposites, such as day and night, man and woman, or light and darkness. However, if one attempts to understand things beyond opposites — thoughts or ideas — the mind may cease to work.

We know how we are born and how we die: we are conceived when two gametes carrying specific genes meet, and we begin to develop in physical form. When we die, all vital bodily functions cease.

In between the life and death of a person, carnal energy plays its role through the information fixed in the genome. Our physical body is composed of many interrelated systems, including the nervous, reproductive, respiratory, and digestive systems, many of which are dependent on our DNA for their proper functioning. The genome is the complete set of genetic instructions that determine an organism's characteristics, consisting of thousands of genes that contain instructions for the production of proteins that carry out various functions in the body. These proteins are responsible for the development and functioning of various bodily systems, including the immune, nervous, and digestive systems.The genome also regulates gene expression, determining when and how genes are turned on or off. We are programmed to behave in certain ways, as the ultimate goal of the carnal Self is to dominate the entire human system. Through my practical research with Shah Abdul Rasheed, I discovered that carnal energy is only temporary and subject to the cycle of life and death, as it seeks to create copies of itself to ensure its own survival. The individual body of a human dies, but the carnal Self keeps itself alive. The secret of the Singularity remains unfolded with humanity behind this life and death.

The beliefs and practices of worship that are based on thought-creation and imagination are a result of information gained through our carnal selves, but the true nature of reality remains undiscovered. Our carnal Self is never satisfied, not even until our last breath. At times, it may be expressed through intense sexual desire or as tears in our eyes. As we face death, we must confront the pain of our carnal energy, knowing that everything we have developed throughout our life is about to be lost. It is only when we are no longer controlled by our carnal energy that we may find a way back to our true origin. The real essence of our being is active only when we are able to burn away the influence of carnal energy within us.

Upon close observation, it becomes clear that carnal energy has a significant influence on our brains, genders, and physical bodies. Consider a man who finds himself at a crossroads, faced with two paths: one right and the other wrong. Both paths are created by the gradual development of carnal energy into either a carnal Self or a carnal soul. This duality of right and wrong, shaped by carnal energy, is based on the male and female human body pattern.

Now, I invite you to join me on a journey toward the Singularity, where insights are expressed through a single male and female pair. Together, we will explore the depths of this unifying force and unlock its mysteries, transcending the limitations of our carnal selves to reach a higher plane of understanding.

CHAPTER – 2

THE MAP OF THE UNIVERSE IN THE HUMAN BODY

The Big Bang is the result of a materialistic universe, and the physical body of a human is also a product of this materialistic universe. However, the story of mankind predates the Big Bang. The body of the noblest creature contains the map of the living universe, where the Singularity is always alive and is the underlying force behind the universe we observe and study with our external senses. To understand the purpose of all creations, one must seek out the noblest creature, and the purpose and map of the materialistic universe, galaxies, stars, and other creations are stored within mankind, the noblest creation. Although we consider ourselves to be the noblest creation, our physical bodies are greatly influenced by carnal energy. To make our bodies function as the noblest creation, we must recognize and understand the carnal energy and examine how the human body is formed.

As we know, the human body is created through fertilization, where a sperm cell from the male reproductive system combines with an egg cell from the female reproductive system. The origin of human gametes, sperm in males and eggs in females, can be traced back to the process of meiosis.

Meiosis of human gametes occurs in the testes in males and the ovaries in females. During embryonic development, the gonadal ridge develops into the testes, epididymis, and vas deferens in males, and the ovaries, fallopian tubes, and uterus in females. Both the testes and ovaries descend during fetal life, with the testes ultimately descending to the scrotum while the ovaries remain in the pelvis.

Upon closer examination, the origin of the male and female reproductive organs can be found between the floating ribs (eleventh and twelfth ribs) and the spinal cord. The eleventh and twelfth ribs are connected to the body via the vertebrae of the spine. Furthermore, the gametes from which the human body is created have their origin between the floating ribs (eleventh and twelfth ribs) and the backbone. This space is the origin of our reproductive system, where a single fluid exists from which life originates, creating two gametes. This single fluid is the single energy.

Regardless of physical gender, humans develop in two forms: one belonging to carnal energy and the other to a single energy, which represents dark energy for the brain. The point of observation is a space where a single fluid exists from which human gametes have descended, and it functions in two forms. One form represents carnal energy in the shape of a serpent, and the other form represents single energy as a cave of darkness. By default, carnal energy becomes fully activated when the human body receives oxygen and begins functioning through external senses, developing itself as a complete Self that governs the human body. This Self ceases to exist with physical death but can remain alive by creating copies along with copies of human bodies. In some cases, this Self can influence other bodies even after physical death, exerting control through faith, dreams, thoughts, and intellect. Carnal energy also functions in the form of communication from the brain through the spinal cord to all parts of the body, driven by carnal energy. The rare functioning of the human body occurs when it can observe itself without the influence of the Self and the intellect developed by carnal energy. This observation is possible in the space where single fluid exists from which the human body is created, but it must be done through single energy without the influence of carnal energy and its developed Self. When carnal energy is active and controlling the human body, everything is observed through external senses and external light, including the light generated within the human body by carnal energy. It is an active serpent that produces venom to control the human brain and, consequently, the entire system of the human body.

The observation begins by watching the communication between the brain and different parts of the body, starting specifically at the place where the gametes have descended. When observation is made without the influence of carnal energy, the carnal energy appears as a serpent entering a dark tunnel, trapped in a cave of darkness with a closed exit gate. As it enters, it loses its physical form and becomes a matter of a single eye. Here, the observer is the single eye without any physical body, overseeing its own existence. The active serpent, in its full form, is now completely surrounded by darkness, confined within the cave of darkness. It becomes only a single eye surrounded by darkness and nothingness, a single dark matter in a realm of darkness. This tiny dark matter is the living and watchful essence of darkness and nothingness facing the closed gate. The arrival of night brings the first sound as the night comer knocks on the exit gate from outside. The piercing star breaks through the darkness with its penetrating rays of light. This eye receives the rays and absorbs them.

After absorbing the rays, the single eye becomes heated with energy from the piercing star. It becomes so hot that it has the potential to create something One can realize how the universe came into existence. The cave in which the carnal energy is trapped is open on one side, and the piercing star penetrates the cave with its rays, opening the other side of the cave. After receiving the rays and the activation from single energy, the single eye embarks on a journey through the human hole. The sign of this human hole in the human body is the formation of a neural tube.

The point of observation that provided light to the single eye now guides the human brain. This is the guidance from the Singularity. Now, this individual observes the external world with the insight of the Singularity. The insight of the Singularity enters into another physical body through the act of observing another person's eyes. It is akin to planting a seed of the Singularity, providing it with water and sunlight, and in this way, the Singularity is always witnessed as alive by the noblest creature.

Chapter – 3

THE SINGLE PAIR

The Single Pair is the only pair in the entire universe capable of both listening and watching the oneness of the Singularity. Upon closer observation, our physical bodies came into existence due to the pairing of gametes (egg and sperm), just as the Singularity also used its own pair for the evolution of the universe through the act of seeing and hearing. The purpose of this evolution is to create a Single Speaking Speaker who serves as a witness to the Singularity among all of creation.

While we are familiar with physical pairs, such as male and female, and the physical and emotional desires that bind them, humankind's origin stems from a single pair of male and female. Our physical bodies are the result of a process involving two gametes that become an embryo and develop into an infant, but the creation of a single pair of male and female does not necessarily indicate the creation of physical bodies. It is important to recognize this creation, as it may lead us to understand the purpose of human existence on Earth.

Humanity only reflects its true nature when it reaches the pinnacle of nobility among all creatures. To achieve this, we must overcome the influence of carnal energy within the human body.

The carnal Self, as it develops in human bodies, creates its copies and divides itself into male and female counterparts. Its development is dependent on how humans are used in the present time. Carnal energy is able to generate more energy which determines the future of carnal energy in future generations. Differently developed carnal selves create different forms of carnal energy. The carnal Self develops and acts as a burning fire in the body. This energy is consumed differently in different bodies, and a person dies as soon as this energy is completely consumed. However, the copy of energy is ready to function in other bodies. It divides itself into male and female counterparts. The inherent opposition fixed between these male and female bodies creates an attraction by using the brain, leading to the continuous cycle of birth and death of carnal energy.

The entire process of carnal energy is orchestrated by a queen of the human genome who serves as the source of all carnal energy and facilitates the fusion of two gametes. The origin of the human genome is that single queen whose impression is imprinted on every human body. The one who can recognize this queen, regardless of physical gender, gains the ability to shape their own destiny. A partial example of this can be seen in queen bees, where offspring are produced through parthenogenesis. In parthenogenesis, the offspring develop from unfertilized eggs and typically inherit all their genetic material from a single parent. Unfertilized eggs develop into males, which are haploid and have half the number of chromosomes, while fertilized eggs develop into females, which are diploid. Furthermore, queen bee pheromones play a crucial role in communication and coordination within the honeybee colony. Similarly, the queen of the human genome produces carnal energy that influences the behavior, physiology, and reproductive processes of all human bodies.

The queen of the human genome herself is devoid of any desire, and her ultimate aim is to manifest a body that reflects the insight of the Singularity. Through that body, the queen gets dissolved along with it in the Singularity. That queen is a single female without a body, and the one who recognizes her in a body is a single male. The single male and female don't operate like physical bodies. The meeting of that pair is a sign of singularity. After their meeting, the Single Speaking One can speak in physical form as well. That single speaking receives guidance from the Singularity. That Single Speaking One is also the only one in the entire universe and the same for all creations. The Single Pair is the only one of its kind in the entire universe, consisting of a male and a female. After their meeting, that pair is now a speaking one who bears witness to the Singularity. The darkness listens to the single eye, and the eye watches the darkness. The pair are constantly observing and listening, and the entire universe speaks to them because they have sacrificed themselves to bear witness to the Singularity.

The Singularity exists everywhere, and nothing is parallel to it. We are here on this Earth because of the Singularity, and nature has blessed mankind with the ability to understand it. No creation can become the Singularity; it is constantly alive, creating space, atoms, and energy. To understand it, one must seek the guidance of someone who already knows it, as observing it without such guidance is impossible.

I strongly believe that this realization has the potential to greatly impact our future as a species. It is an exploration of the ethical and practical implications of altering the very fabric of our being.

CHAPTER – 4

A JOURNEY OF DISCOVERY WITH SHAH RASHEED AND URFI JAN

Since childhood, I have been searching for answers to the mysteries of life, death, and the force behind the entire universe. It was in May 2014 when I met Shah Abdul Rashid at my home as he was invited by my father. My first eye contact with Shah Rasheed and his profound words about the true essence of a person struck me deeply.

In November 2014, I went to a place called Ashmuqam in Kashmir, where Shah Rasheed spent most of his time conducting practical classes with his disciples. It was there that I met a young lady named Urfi Jan, who sat beside Shah Rasheed and supported him on the path of truthfulness. Together, they transcended gender biases and worked together to alter the influence of carnal energy on human bodies. Since then, I have been spending most of my time with Shah Rasheed and Urfi Jan.

Since May 2014, I have documented my findings and realizations. These are firsthand experiences that I have lived and witnessed.

Through my interactions with Urfi Jan, I discovered that she lived a normal life before meeting Shah Rasheed. However, their encounter sparked a transformation within her, bringing forth her true inner Self in physical form. Urfi Jan met Shah Rasheed in 2010. I found in her something that touched her deeply, for which she has sacrificed her routine life.

I closely observed their relationship and realized that both of them were living a life that went beyond the influence of carnal energy. In front of them, I realized that there is an identity of mankind that is beyond physical appearance and gender differences. Shah Rasheed emphasized the significance of two gametes and their origin. With his guidance, it became clear that one can realize any energy within the human body when they are prepared to face it.

In the initial stages, people in their surroundings objected to Urfi's decision to depart from the normal routine of life, and she faced numerous challenges. Nevertheless, her ultimate goal of realizing the essence of life remained her top priority.

Shah's guidance has influenced many lives, altering their very being and aligning them with the functioning of the Singularity within their physical bodies. As he said, there are various types of genes in the human genome.The first gene or instruction of the Singularity must be activated and dominated within the human body to attain its purpose. Nature follows a process and does not favor interference. The human body has altered energy in such a way that it now works against the fundamental principles of nature. It is crucial for individuals to introspect and consider what legacy we are leaving behind for future generations. This energy was there for a positive purpose to create the physical bodies of humans to know the Singularity, but this energy is being altered during the living life of humans.

We exist because of our ancestors, and when our present is on the right path, our future will also be in the right direction. According to Shah Rasheed, the millions of sperms and thousands of eggs within human bodies are witnessing that some living beings are attempting to inhabit human bodies. However, they are unable to do so because something has gone wrong with the carriers in the past. These living beings are functional in us, but they don't have physical forms like us. But indirectly, they influence our personality and work against us.We are also carrying future generations within us. We have the power to correct them within this single body we possess right now. This life does not solely belong to us but to all of humanity. Each being bears responsibility and will be held accountable for their actions. The energy altered by human bodies controls the deeds we perform.

Engaging in bodily worship or pursuing desires gives life to the carnal energy. Like any worship done with breathing, meditating on any part of the body, keeping attention toward any person, and guidance through dreams or thoughts leads to mismanagement of the human body. It creates negative forces in human bodies. This is very drastic for all of humanity. The human has only a single sign which needs to be observed under proper guidance for exploring the different dimensions of humanity. The carnal energy especially requires the touch of the Singularity, where all beings are equal and originate from the same source. This touch is from the Creator of everything and does not have any bodily desire. The witness of the Singularity can only manifest through the human body, having single guidance. We must simply observe the role given to us in this life and how we fulfill it.

CHAPTER – 5

MEDITATION BY CARNAL ENERGY

Meditation is a deliberate and structured practice that involves training the mind and cultivating specific qualities of awareness, focus, and relaxation. During meditation, individuals typically sit in a comfortable position, close their eyes, and direct their attention to a specific point of focus, such as their breath, a mantra, a visual image, or bodily sensations.

Sometimes, meditation also involves being fully present and aware of what is happening in the present moment without judgment or attachment. However, this awareness is primarily focused on carnal energy and strives to be in the present moment. Meditation is an intentional and structured practice that requires dedicated time for focused attention. It specifically refers to the training of the mind and the cultivation of specific qualities through dedicated techniques.

The flow of carnal energy through various points in the human body is influenced by meditation. The human body is designed in a functional manner from head to toe, and understanding the flow and impact of this energy, in conjunction with meditation, is essential to explore its effects on individuals and future generations.

In some cases, a meditation practice starts from the pelvic plexus at the base of the spine, where the carnal energy manifests as a serpent-like force. From the base of the spine, it rises to the hypogastric plexus, continues its ascent to the solar plexus, cardiac plexus, and carotid plexus, and it finally reaches the medulla.At the medulla, the energy further ascends to the crown of the head, interacting with the glands and influencing the brain. This energy exhibits a duality, presenting itself as half male and half female.

Upon reaching the glands in the head, a unique phenomenon occurs that surpasses the practitioner's control. This practice can lead to hormonal imbalances, and at this stage, the energy may seek another physical body to move out or cause harm to the current body. In some cases, this half-male and half-female energy creates an artificial oneness within a single body through self-fulfilling desire. Consequently, the body becomes entangled in the consumption of this carnal energy, resulting in profound challenges for future generations.

Partially activated energy at different points or fully activated energy, when practiced again, perpetuates the cycle of consumption and entrapment. Despite the initial perception of this energy activation as spiritual enlightenment, a closer examination reveals its profound negative consequences. Individuals become trapped within the intricate web of carnal energy, unknowingly perpetuating the cycle of consumption and entrapment. Many individuals claiming to be spiritual healers or sages are actually products of this carnal energy, leaving a dark mark on humanity.

True enlightenment begins with observing the origin of human gametes, free from the influence of carnal energy. It is through this observation that the true journey of mankind begins.

Damage occurs due to incorrect or misguided practices promoted in the name of spiritual awakening. These practices involve meditation with breathing and paying attention to specific objects, body parts, or individuals, leading to narcissism.

When encountering individuals who display narcissistic traits within spiritual or sage-like roles, it is important for followers or seekers to exercise discernment and critical thinking. It is advisable to maintain a balanced perspective, question and verify teachings, and prioritize the well-being of humanity.

CHAPTER – 6

THE HUMAN HOLE: A JOURNEY TOWARD SINGULARITY

The human body exhibits a clear indication of possessing a hole or tunnel that transcends the constraints of time and space. It is a single piece of information fused within our bodies that shapes human intellect and distinguishes us from other species. This human intellect is influenced by singularity rather than carnal energy. While we existed even before the meeting of gametes, the proper communication system was absent until the formation of a complete physical body.

The creator of the Singularity formed a complete, fused pair having the ability to listen and observe. The pair exists in separate stages. One represents a singular piece of information, while the other embodies its corresponding matter. When united, they fuse together without any interval. This singular pair serves as a witness to the Singularity and remains in constant communication with its creator, always watchful and attentive.

The act of witnessing the Singularity evoked a desire to speak, resulting in the pair's separation fueled by envy. This envy has now transformed into an energy. Utilizing this energy, the separated pair generates numerous additional pairs with the sole purpose of creating a single speaking witness. One part of the original pair remains in the initial stage, existing merely as an informational component within creations, while the other is utilized to create a vast creation in the form of matter.

The component in the first stage remains active, possessing a singular piece of information about its creator, and resides as a fragment of knowledge within human bodies. However, the other component became deeply entangled in the influence of carnal energy, leading it to exist in a state of lost humanity. This lost component also represents singularity within all of mankind.

While the component in the first stage continues to observe, the component existing as matter serves as a listener. The influence of carnal energy on matter has caused it to lose its consciousness of listening. The ultimate objective of these creations is to first become a singular matter devoid of the influence of carnal energy and then to listen to what the other component is seeing.

This can only be achieved through a tunnel from which this pair emerged into the realm of matter, transcending the constraints of time.

This human body is designed to reach singularity through its singular information, which is stored within our bodies and functions through the central nervous system and its communication routes. Accessing this singular information requires surpassing the barriers of carnal energy, and it serves as a universal guide toward singularity.

Let us examine our central nervous system, including the brain and spinal cord. The central nervous system (CNS) serves as the command center of the body, coordinating and regulating various bodily functions. It receives, processes, and transmits information throughout the body, controlling bodily functions, facilitating cognitive processes, and enabling movement. The neural tube, a crucial structure in embryonic development, eventually develops into the nervous system, including the brain and spinal cord.

The formation of the neural tube begins with the neural plate, which undergoes a process called neural groove formation. The neural plate invaginates, creating a groove along its central axis that deepens over time. The elevated edges of the neural groove, known as neural folds, eventually fuse at the midline. Fusion starts in the middle of the embryo and progresses toward both ends, marking the closure of the neural tube. The cranial end gives rise to future brain structures, while the caudal end forms the future spinal cord. The elongation and differentiation of the caudal end result in spinal cord segments responsible for transmitting signals between the brain and the body.

The fusion of the neural folds gives rise to the neural tube, and some cells from the edges of the neural folds break away to form the neural crest. The neural tube and the fusion signify the role of the human hole, driven by singular information. The complete body's journey is guided by carnal energy, which also plays a role in forming the physical body. However, mankind has become overly influenced by this bodily energy, and it is now working against the collective interests of humanity. The purpose of this human body is not solely to fulfill bodily desires but to understand and discover the Singularity. Nature creates human bodies through a process, but it also destroys them through a process.

The journey toward the human hole commences when the carnal energy, which influences the CNS, including the brain and spinal cord, loses its energy and transforms into a single exotic matter. This matter defies the laws of science, possessing the potential to travel and remain intact without collapse.

Human intelligence consists of a solitary piece of information stored within the human body. Among all creations and species, only the human body is intricately designed so that this singular information becomes active within the human hole—the tunnel within the human body.

The sign of this tunnel within our body is the neural tube, which contains this singular piece of information and now functions as the CNS. This information or guidance is the same for all individuals living in this world. By diminishing the influence of carnal energy, it becomes possible to access the singular information related to singularity. However, this singular information can only move with a singular matter when the closed sides of the tunnel are opened. Nature repeats this process continuously. The human hole is created with the sole purpose of meeting the Singularity. It is not a theoretical hole or tunnel; it functions as intended by its creator.

LOVE FOR ONENESS

The Singularity in love with love,
Falls for its own reflection thereof,
As lover and beloved meet in union,
Witnessing oneness, a divine communion.

Through creations, the Singularity speaks,
Of its own unity, the truth it seeks,
Always alive, always living,
Infinite love, boundless and giving.

Watching and listening to its pair,
Singularity creates, driven by care,
Dissolving into the beloved, it melds,
Their union, creating everything that swells.

Physical form, carnal energy,
Their meeting creates a symphony,
The Singularity in darkness to comprehend,
But to the pair, a star burning to no end.

Infinite, the Singularity shines,
Giving light and life to all divine,
Love, the force that drives it on,
Eternal, immortal, never gone.

Shah Abdul Rasheed

Urfi Jan

"I am eternally grateful for the kind and beautiful hearts of my cherished mentors."

– Muhammad Umran

www.ingramcontent.com/pod-product-compliance
Lightning Source LLC
LaVergne TN
LVHW091243150826
845673LV00003B/1276

* 9 7 9 8 8 9 0 2 6 8 7 7 8 *